40 DAYS TO EMOTIONAL FREEDOM

A step by step guidebook

Healing the past and reconnecting

To peace, joy, love, and purpose

MARYANNE RODGERS

DEDICATION

To all who not only wish to be free,

but find the courage to face themselves,

and walk boldly out into the light.

CONTENTS

ACKNOWLEDGMENTS

I would like to thank God for leading me through my own dark places, bringing me out healed and changed and then inspiring me to share this journey with others. To my friends and family for their support throughout this project, particularly my husband Randy for believing in me. To Lisa my sister for inspiring me. To Wendy my Life Coach and friend for her support and encouragement. And to Chuckles our dog, who patiently lay beside me during hours of writing.
I am truly blessed beyond words.

INTRODUCTION

This is a self-help book for people who like short winded, get to the point stuff.

Who has time for 300 pages these days? Me neither, so I wrote a book that anyone can easily follow, with real practical steps you can work through day by day, bringing lasting changes in your emotional life and beyond.

Written as a guide style, workbook, each day has a topic and suggested steps to follow. Designed as a tool to get you talking and unlock hidden issues, detoxify negative emotions, re-think limiting beliefs, bring healing, reconnection to self, then rebuilding in many different areas. Think of it as a spring cleaning for your emotions, cleansing your inner life; giving you more peace and joy and for some even clarifying direction along the way. This will be a unique journey specific to you, your life experiences and emotional healing needs, with results that may surprise you- it will be worth it, I promise!

My Story
I had a choice...

Stay the same (easy) doesn't require anything new or different, keep on breathing inhale, exhale and repeat.

Or... change!

Oh...Where would I start, what would I do?

For me there was a subtle sadness, under the surface mostly in the form of self-pity or self-criticism. I felt stuck, unconsciously going through the motions but inwardly desperate for change. My past still had a negative influence on me and I remained trapped in unhealthy patterns of thinking; filtering life through those past experiences. Some other circumstances were changing, I wasn't particularly happy with my life at the time, and it was all something of a perfect storm that had me asking the question: "what is up with this?"

Funny how it can take years (or even decades) of the same stuff repeating itself to realize it isn't going to change on its own- or with time *or* even maturity.

How annoying! Couldn't I just be happy for a change? And for longer than an afternoon at a time...mornings were out for me (getting out of bed was something like raising the dead) and evenings seemed to be spent anxiously contemplating the next day. Everything had to be so finely balanced to be happy and it didn't go deep- like I imagined it could.

I had sprinklings of good times, usually involving a new purchase, tequila or cheesecake- you get the idea. That's not lasting as we all know (getting new stuff, any outside additive only mask the symptoms) I wanted a little lasting contentment and peace.

A little background...

I was 39 and ½, married to a good man- we had met 6 years previous, and been married for almost 5 years. Admittedly I was one of those "obsessed about marriage girls" who put way too much pressure on a relationship and marriage to fulfill me- which no other human can possibly do. I had learnt first-hand that we drag our stuff into the marriage and then wonder why the other person can't fix or heal us.

I had a good job in the corporate world, but found things slowing down after a few steady years. Could I keep myself fully engaged? Was this what I wanted to do for the rest of my life? Everything I touched began to fall apart, so much so it was almost comical. It certainly worked at getting my attention- okay I'm listening now!

We didn't have any children, after wavering on the decision it was made for us in the form of a partial hysterectomy. The exhaustion from the operation certainly didn't help matters, and some days I dreamt of doing absolutely nothing.

A couple of months later we adopted a 4 month old puppy from the local shelter, surprisingly unclaimed. We walked in on a stormy spring Sunday and fell in love. My husband took a little longer, until the minute "Chuckles" we later named him, fell on his back and begged for a belly rub. So cute- he is something of a Maltese, Poodle mix (and yes I am one of those obnoxious pet owners that will show you pictures on my phone). My heart opened up, like only an animal lover can truly understand.

It was only a month after this event that I began this process work on my inner life.

Physically I was in shoulder and neck pain from years at a computer, in a somewhat stressful environment, so around that same time I began fairly intense restorative chiropractic treatment that helped greatly in the healing process with my body. So things were looking up!

Your heart is bleeding for me right now- isn't it? I mean- please!
I know, I almost wish I had some story overcoming incredible odds of
survival or something. Well there were a few traumatic years early on, if
that makes you feel any better. But I thought it helpful to paint an
accurate picture of where I was at the time- when I began to face my
stuff. It was a fairly typical suburban rut of same-y sameness with
underlying pain, which was either going to spark a revolution, *or*
possibly a plunge into prescription drug use (or whatever else I could
do with the least amount of guilt or illegality).

Covering the symptoms…(easier than figuring out the cause)
So I did try a brief stint on anti-depressants, my doctor recommended a
therapist in conjunction with a low dose prescription -a few days later I
made the call.
At the other end I was greeted with the question: "what would you like
to see me about?" I was caught off guard, (I didn't expect her to ask
me questions until we were in person) it was like a scene from a movie,
as I stuttered down the phone in whispers, ah… well… I… ah…then
used the excuse about being at work and not being able to talk.
At the time I wasn't able to articulate what I needed to say, that I
needed something, someone to talk to, that I was unhappy, or stuck or
whatever it was and I certainly didn't want to confess I was depressed-
that just sounded too extreme. Anyway short story short, we didn't end
up meeting; after a couple more rounds of phone tag- final score 0.
One of us didn't follow through -probably me.
So I had finally joined the club. Everyone was on something these
days, the world had seemingly gone pill-popping mad. I was a small
walking (over the counter) pharmacy at the time myself-nothing major
just armed and ready. Heaven forbid we feel pain, let's not actually feel
anything too much- right? Emotional pain can be as bad as physical
pain and can continue untreated for years; a constant nagging, joy
robbing sucker, plus you have to take a good amount of something to
get deep enough to really numb that emotional stuff.
I didn't stay on the anti-depressants for long as they seemed to
make me swing in either direction (what goes up must come down)
then someone gets it, usually my nearest and dearest. Plus I quickly
realized I wanted to get to the cause, not cover the symptoms. (No
judgment for anyone on anti-depressants).

Disclaimer: *Obviously I am not suggesting any changes to any prescription or medication currently taken- please consult your doctor regarding any medical advice. This book does not claim to treat any medical condition.*

Then I thought about trying another therapist but reasoned: what if I talked and *I* listened? Since I knew me anyway, it would sure save a lot of "getting to know ya details" I was happy to skip (since I had heard it all before). Seeking therapy is an excellent plan for many people and I highly recommend it, the very act of talking to someone with an unbiased perspective is reason alone. It just wasn't the road for me at the time.

Back to my story...
I was now 39 and 3/4 quarters, staring down the barrel of my 40th birthday knowing some of my "stuff" wasn't welcome in the next season of life.
To be honest it started with vanity, or we could say "health." I had gained a few pounds after the hysterectomy together with my sedentary office job over the past few years. With my birthday looming only a few short months away, I became determined to make some changes. I didn't want to weigh the same, look the same (in case we threw a big party) or more importantly *feel* the same.
After shedding a few pounds, I was feeling better on the outside and now needed to lighten up on the inside. I became suddenly motivated to shed whatever else was weighing me down before June (it was April). A little sense of urgency seemed to help and I was finally fully onboard with the process!

Running towards it (a fresh approach)
I knew I had to face my stuff.
So ignoring my prior beliefs about not looking inward or focusing too much on self. I figured doing it didn't mean I had to talk about it for the rest of my life or anything, let's just go there, face it, get free and move on!
Basically I was that matter of fact about it.
So one day I started- like a detective digging around looking for what was hidden in the dark corners; those little thorns hiding in my soul. Whatever I could find that was better out than in, I was finally willing to handle.

To be honest my expectations weren't that high, I really just wanted some of the history recordings to stop playing over and over-that alone would be awesome.

I had no idea doing this work would show me that I could completely change my life.

Noticeable changes...
This is working!

Fairly quickly, I noticeably felt like the inside *was* beginning to change and soften.

What I began to discover was the inner whining, cynicism, self-pity, blaming and even fears- got quieter. I was impulse-shopping, sleeping, eating, and drinking less, without even trying (my preferred forms of self-soothing). Impulses were softening, compassion grew, I was okay being alone and I noticed an improvement when it came to listening to others, (always room for improvement there). Empathy grew, I was no longer just in my own head replaying my own sad story as someone was sharing theirs; I was truly engaging and more able to feel for *them*.

Starting to wake up...
I became much more aware of my thoughts and choice of words, like someone had turned up the volume on me, showing me the connection between what I was putting out and getting back- literally creating my own future with. I became more open and hungry for positivity in my life, even things I had previously criticized I began to embrace.

Some other interesting things happened: increased confidence and clarity about my own direction and purpose in life followed this work. My whole life started to change little by little every day as the load lightened. That subtle sadness I was so familiar with left and it was like the sun came out.

No coincidences...
And then something else interesting happened: I became aware of people around me having similar struggles.

My interest at the time was particularly about "life purpose," and in the course of talking to people about finding their purpose in life, I discovered a startling connection to the need for inner healing, often *before* their purpose could be clearly realized. It was like skipping the most important part. What had worked for me could also work for others, since I had discovered my purpose after doing this work, maybe it was the missing piece to the puzzle?

This book became something I *had* to do, after I heard the question: "how do I get free- I don't know how?"

So I put together the same process work that I have done, polished it up and added some things I learned even as this book was coming together, which I am now excited to share with you.

Go for it...

I recognize talking about emotions isn't exactly something most of us would *prefer* to do. It is usually perceived as a weakness, but in reality it takes true inner strength to even pick up a book like this.

Most people react with: "get over it" "deal with it" but very little seems to be available on the actual "how to" _how_ do you deal with emotional pain? "How do you get free?"

We all, well most of us want to be free, and we want to "get over it" right? But do we want to *really* go there? Hell NO!

Well I hate to break it to you but you *are* going there anyway- by *not* going there, so why not really go there and not have to visit anymore. The problem is internal, it can't be fixed with external things, we need to go in. Avoidance doesn't work, neither does suppression, running or a quick fix...of any kind. Sorry –I almost wish it did, it would sure make life a lot easier.

If we do nothing- the pain continues and we keep the emotional bags as long as we want, our whole life if we do nothing about it. Ever been stuck traveling with a really heavy bag? You wish you had one with wheels, and your shoulder throbs after about 5 minutes of lugging it around. Imagine unloading some of that stuff or even better- all of it.

Maybe the word "bag" is not working here- I am not talking about Gucci, Prada, or Coach (insert favorite designer here), I am talking about stinky, gross garbage bags the kind that you can't get to the trash quick enough before the stuff leaks out. They are the emotional bags we carry around subconsciously or consciously and hope nobody will notice. Well woodland creatures know, as well as the highly evolved male/female you might like to date (so if that isn't reason enough to make a change). A little extra motivation never hurt. Or if a hot date is not on your agenda put whatever else you would like *or* like to change in this space.....

Feelings (your navigation system)

So let's shift the focus, for these 40 days and start to work on the stuff that is weighing you down and holding you back…and see where you go. For the next 40 days be more aware of your thoughts and feelings listen to them and acknowledge them through this work. Your feelings are actually your God-given navigation system, there to direct you through life. I don't mean: "do you feel like getting out of bed," kind of feelings. More on an intuitive gut level: I feel like I should go back to college or I feel bad every time I hang out with that person, or I feel like I need to move to Greenland (now that would take a strong feeling, to live above the Arctic Circle) but you get my point.

Misery loves -well misery…

This work won't be particularly easy, but neither is life so you are well prepared. Actually the harder you find it, the greater your life change will be at the completion of the process. The hardest part is getting *still* to do the work: the assignments themselves are not difficult.

You do need to be ready and willing to let go of your misery. This may sound ridiculous but many people are very comfortable in their misery and don't want to change- we meet them all the time. Plus it gives them an excuse for their behavior. So be honest about it, if you go at this work defensively it may not help you if you go through every day of this process thinking "that's not me," so be as open as you can.

I broke it into small bites for each day, understanding that life must go on in the middle of this and so not to be too overwhelming for anyone. You may find some days harder than others, don't quit on yourself. If you don't feel you can't tackle a particular topic, don't pressure yourself, just start talking it through and give yourself time to process.

A couple of things you will need:

> ✓ Notebook or paper and pen (or you can type it out on your computer)
> ✓ A quiet calm environment
> ✓ Honesty and sincerity to each assignment

Don't worry no one will be grading you or reviewing your responses and you can't fail.

Some days may touch on repeat issues for you, or cross over that's okay, just continue on or skip if you feel no connection (emotional charge or reaction) to a certain issue.

You may feel a little more tired than usual (especially during the "Detox" section) so be aware of that. Self-soothing habits may be triggered more than usual while going through the steps, do your best to make healthy choices but don't focus on that, this process will still work. Be careful making any rash life changing decisions while doing this work, give yourself enough time to fully process.

Distractions and procrastination (Cousin Kiki)
Be aware of the possibility of a plethora of excuses coming up for why going to cousin Kikis' Tupperware party is more important. Just sayin'- to be aware, while this work is good for the soul, you may want to subconsciously avoid it. It will take a little determination as your inner critic (ego) will probably try and convince you this is a waste of time- don't listen. Once you get into it, it should get easier as you connect more with your true self. Anything hidden has power, as we expose this stuff and bring it into the light, it will lessen its power over your life.

Open to interpretation (yours)
This is just a guide, feel free to add or take away from my suggestions. This is to serve you as a guide, we are all at different stages of our journey and I respect that. There is plenty of room for personal interpretation for each day- it is really to get you talking, and go where you need to go.
I did try to be thorough, but realize this process may not cover everything for everybody. I think you will be surprised how much gets covered and more excitingly, what this heals for you and leads you to. You might prefer to process in a slightly different way to my suggested (writing it out) you could also; talk it out, paint/draw, pray, meditate- whatever feels right for you.

Each day, I will give you a place to start and finish, what you do in the middle is specific to you it's your journey- there is no right or wrong here. The more you actually *do* this work, and not just read through it- the better. If something is being triggered- tackle it, don't be afraid to go there and let yourself process until you feel clear and at peace about it. The most important thing is to get the pain out, anything after that is a plus. Strengthening your thoughts is next and we talk about that. I do repeat myself throughout this process in some regards, it is for a reason- we usually don't get things the first time.

What you do with the rest is personal to you, I will ask questions (to get you thinking) and make some suggestions, but it is up to you. If you want to destroy what you write, or keep it- your choice.

From flabby to fabulous (building mental strength)
I include some basic "affirmations" for some of the days, I prefer to call them "declarations" because affirmations sometimes get a bad rap- usually by negative people but they do work. They may sound foreign at first, even a little crazy but they are just *tools* or you could call them: mental strengthening devices. They work so well to reprogram and counteract the negative thoughts that traffic through our heads. I relied on them heavily for 6 months because I was so darn negative, I still do but now it is way more natural to be positive. Affirmations should be authentic and sound real/believable to you, that will happen the more you hear yourself say them, feel free to come up with your own as well. They are not a one-time thing and work the more you use them. You are not lying to yourself; you are doing a mental work-out and building some muscle where there used to be flab- mental flab. You can be smart but flabby. Well educated but flabby, physically ripped but mentally flabby. By the end of this journey you may have some guns- mental guns to shoot down the wrong thoughts that keep you stuck. (That's for the guys that think this subject is wimpy or just for girls). *When* you do this is up to you whatever time of day that works best, you decide.

How long will each of these take? I don't really want to put a time limit/expectation on it, some days will be about half an hour, or less. Others may take longer depending on how deep you want to go or need to go, obviously the more time you can give to this the better.

Let's get started...
Shift into an offensive attitude towards this work, not a defensive one this is important work; you are essentially setting yourself free.
Isn't it time for more joy, and peace in your life and less turmoil?
Haven't you lost enough time dwelling on what you can't change, wouldn't it be better to focus on what you can? So let's get started...

We need to go *within*, so we no longer go *without…*

DETOX – Section 1

This first section is "detoxifying days," dealing with and releasing negative emotions. Each day has rebuilding components also to help you to travel light.

Day 1- Commitment to Yourself

Welcome to this 40 day journey!

Try to enjoy the journey and focus on the benefits of self-exploration through each day instead of only on the final destination.

Most of us are in some kind of a truce with ourselves, we may have given up the war, but now it is time to get on the same team...

In your own words, write a commitment to yourself while going through this process.

Perhaps come up with a reward you could give yourself at the end if that works for you?

In your own words...Hello soul...

(You can sign your name if you like).

Day 2- Sadness to Joy

Take a few deep slow breaths, and relax your whole body.

Today we are going to get started by talking about sadness.

Begin to think about anything from your past that may still be affecting you.

What thoughts make you sad from your past?

What thoughts make you sad or unhappy in your present?

Do your best to get as much out as you can, in detailed dialog or in list form, however you would prefer: you can write it out or talk it out.

Really engage with yourself, hear yourself, feel the feelings and face them with courage. If something painful comes up, let it come.

Consider... (If you aren't sure where to start)

Do you get hung up on disappointments from the past?

Do you dwell on what could have been?

Have you lost hope?

When you are done writing or talking, accept what you wrote by making peace with it and choosing to be okay with what is, what was and what you are powerless to change.

Accept what *was* and give up the need to have it be any other way. Let it go.

Forgive yourself (if you didn't in your writing). In your own words...

Forgive anyone else you may need to forgive (which you do for yourself). That does not mean you *agree* or *approve* of what happened it is *acceptance* of what was and letting go of the *possibility* of it being any different.

Rebuilding

- Move towards joy in your life. You can choose it on purpose, which creates more of it (the best way to create it, is to give it to others) make someone else happy and you will be too.
- When you are tempted to think thoughts of sadness, or complain about your life, make another choice. Imagine negative thoughts are little bugs, lets say something like ants (not too creepy) scurrying around in your head that you don't want; when you think more productive, positive thoughts it stops the bugs (or kills them if you prefer). Become a bug zapper!
- Be thankful every day, even if you have to start with: "I have air to breathe." Thankfulness shifts you into a different mental pattern (instead of being stuck in what is wrong or missing).
- The majority of sadness is self-pity which is very destructive, easy to fall into and not even realize. If this is something you find yourself falling into, try allowing yourself 1-5 minutes per day for self-pity and none the rest of the time (as a way to train yourself out of it). Work towards a "no wallowing zone."
- For the next few days especially: choose upbeat positive music, inspiring books, movies or television shows that make you feel good.
- Do you have any future plans you are excited about? If not, maybe you could plan something to do that will give you something fun to look forward to.

Breathing exercise: Use your imagination here to help you. Close your eyes and imagine sadness empting out of you with each breath out, and joy filling you back up with each breath in. Do that for a couple of minutes and feel the shift as heaviness lifts and joy bubbles into every cell of your body.

Affirmations: I am thankful for everything in my life. Joy is growing in my life. I create more joy every day. I give joy to others. I choose to be happy on purpose. I focus on what is good in my life.

*Grief

If you have recently lost a loved one and are in the middle of the grieving process move through it naturally. Many believe the soul chooses when it departs, which isn't our choice as the ones left behind, but it can help us to more graciously accept it by honoring their journey however short their time may have been.

If it has been a long time and you feel stuck in the grief, maybe you could write a parting letter to sadness and grief?

Example: in honor of … (Loved one's name)… I am leaving you sadness, not because I don't love … (Loved one)… and always will, but out of my love for him/her, I leave sadness behind. I am moving forward with courage and leave the mourning behind, moving forward and giving myself permission to be happy and remembering the good memories in honor of … (loved one)…(add anything else you would like to say)

Day 3- Anger to Peace

Welcome to day 3.

Get comfortable, slow your breathing and take some long deep breaths before you begin.

Today we are going to discuss anger, and frustration.

Are you angry about something or at someone from your past that you haven't been able to let go of?

Write or talk on the subject of anger, don't be afraid of this one- Anger is okay, but it's better out than in. Maybe start with frustration, if that is easier. Under anger is hurt and fear, so work through the anger to the hurt underneath.

Give yourself a voice, really hear yourself, and face it with courage. Allow anything painful to come up, drop your guard and let the hurt speak.

Thoughts to consider… (if nothing instantly comes to mind).

What about your life frustrates you right now?

What gets you angry or upset?

Do you feel like a victim in your life or stuck in some way?

Are you angry at someone in particular?

Do you get angry easily?

When you are done writing or talking it out, sit with it for a minute and make peace with it. By accepting what is, what you can't change and give up the need for it to have turned out any other way.

Now release it, let it go, the pain of it, and release the need to hang onto it. In your own words: I release anger and frustration over...

Forgive yourself.

Forgive anyone else you need to forgive.

Forgiveness doesn't mean you *approve or agree* with what happened- but that you *accept* it (that is a subtle but important difference).

Rebuilding

- If you were treated badly or abused in some way, it is normal to be ticked-off about it. When did you get a chance to truly vent or deal with it? As a society we are not very good at allowing or knowing how to deal with anger, so it usually gets suppressed. A good way to release anger is to punch a pillow, or a boxing bag. The action itself helps to identify what you are feeling as it gets released. Feel free to shout and yell as you punch the pillow. You don't have to shout to express anger necessarily, but it can be a great way of releasing the toxic energy from your body and emotions.
  *NB: If you feel yourself boiling in future: punch a pillow and release the negative energy- in the privacy of your own home (don't waste it on the freeway). That energy can make us sick if held onto, so get it out in a safe controlled way.

- Another option is to reason it out: write your frustrations or things that make you angry into short list form and beside each one note: A, B, C, D or E.
  - o A) I let this anger go and let go of control.
  - o B) The situation will change in time: I just need to be patient.
  - o C) I can respond better instead of reacting in anger or fear.
  - o D) There is something else I can do about it (offer forgiveness etc.)
  - o E) Another answer you come up with that better fits (as long as it is not "kill 'em and bury the body)."

- Some people recommend channeling anger as a motivational tool, this can work but be careful you aren't bitter towards any person in the process, let it come from a place of gratitude. It's okay to let injustice/anger about starving children motivate you to give; or acknowledge the frustration in your job and let it fuel you to find another one.
- New picture: see yourself responding completely differently the next chance an opportunity to react in anger comes up. Picture yourself taking a breath, collecting your thoughts and calmly communicating without fear.
- Next time someone comes at you aggressively, consider: are they really hurt or afraid and it is coming out as anger instead of communicating how they are feeling? Instead of elevating the situation could you calm them down by offering comfort or reassurance?
- If you have kids, allow them to express anger in a safe controlled way, get them a boxing bag, or enroll them in a martial art, so they can learn how to deal with anger appropriately. Expecting them not to get angry is unrealistic, so let them vent and listen to them (even if you weren't shown the same consideration growing up).

Activation: Imagine you are holding a ball in your hand, (the ball is whatever you are angry about) then do the action of throwing the invisible ball. See it going far away from you and imagine it exploding into a thousand pieces, burning up and vaporizing.

Breathing exercise: Close your eyes and imagine inhaling pure peace and then exhaling anger/hurt; do that for a couple of minutes and fill up on peace.

Feel peace take over and fill you up as it changes your body and mind chemistry.

Affirmations: I am calm. I am at peace with the world. I let go and surrender. I am thankful for peace in my life. I am peaceful and compassionate. I embrace peace. I am cared for. I have enough. I have what I need. The world is a kind place.

Day 4- Fear to Courage (and love)

Take some slow easy deep breaths and relax, get comfortable and begin.

Today we are going to discuss fear and anxiety. Write down your fears and anything that makes you anxious, either in list form or in detailed paragraphs.

Lean into it, feel yourself melt into your fears instead of resisting as you write them out. Exposing them like this can help bring them into perspective.

Consider…

Are you fearful?

Very fearful, sometimes fearful or occasionally cautious?

Do you often wonder: "what if?"

Do you have a phobia?

Rebuilding

- If you have a fear of a particular outcome, try following it through to the worst case scenario. How likely is that to happen? What if it did? Have you made it through a similar situation before?
- Is there something you can proactively do to face or reduce some of your fears? Even if it is baby steps, that could help diminish unrealistic fears:
  - ➢ Fear of heights: go to an indoor rock climbing wall and start with a small climb.
  - ➢ Fear of public speaking: attend Toastmasters (you don't have to speak right away).
  - ➢ Fear of death: read a book about near death experiences.
- Change your perspective, because what you are afraid of someone else likes, so why not act as if. Refuse to feed the fear any longer by giving it thought time.
- There are really only two base emotions: fear or love. All negative emotions track back to fear or anxiety/stress (the manifestation of fear). Really most of life is perception, which is followed by the feelings. You get to choose how to think about anything, either negatively or positively, dark or light, full or empty, gloomy or hopeful- that is up to you.
- It starts with a thought. Are you happy with your typical choice? Listen to yourself today or tomorrow and listen

to how often you think, feel, speak and act out of fear; consider how you can turn it into love, courage and trust. So maybe if we stay as full of love as we can, there will be no room for fear? You could use love or courage as the fear zapper here by choosing it instead.

- What would love sound like, what does it look like? Love lifts, releases, believes, encourages, liberates, trusts, forgives, accepts, is peaceful, compassionate, joyful, kind, generous, affirms, builds others up and is without condition.
Love also may have to help someone out of the comfy nest for their own good, so they can fly.

- Good thoughts create good feelings which create good events, relationships and ultimately a good life, it becomes addictive in a healthy way once you experience how life can suddenly begin to give you blueberries instead of the blues. You get to decide how your life will be, you actually have more power then you may realize. We are constantly sending out little signals of energy and the universe responds in kind (with the same energy) so give it exactly what you want back as it only knows how to copy.

- Release yourself from perceived fears, fear of making a mistake, fear of failure, punishment and release yourself from all self-imposed expectations and limitations. Now say that sentence back in the first person: "I release myself from all perceived fears: fear of making mistakes, fear of failure, or punishment and I release myself from all self-imposed expectations and limitations as well as the expectations or limitations projected onto me by others."

- Deduce fear feeding: consider ignoring the news for a few days or weeks, if you can (the media are trained to feed fear). Limit time with overly negative and fearful people that lock you into a whining session about how bad the world/life is.

- If you have children, speak courage and confidence to your kids, watch the words you choose or they could grow up overly afraid. Parenthood seems to amplify fears but don't let it win! I'm not talking about caution: of course teach them to use caution when crossing the street etc. But don't use fear as a teacher: "that car will squash you like a bug!" There is a difference: we need to teach our kids to be cautious in a balanced way, and not be freaked-out about everything.

- Think of all the ways you have shown courage in your life, consider some of the hard decisions you have made and the bravery you have shown. How have you been courageous?

Breathing exercise: Take a couple of slow breaths and inhale love, feel love fill your lungs, every vein, and go throughout your body. Exhale fear, see it leaving your body and mind. Repeat this for a couple of minutes, as you fill up on love, get full and bask in it. Let all fears and concerns leave your body and mind with each breath as love and trust replaces fear.

Affirmations: I am courageous. I am loved. I am a loving person. I am full of love and courage to face life with confidence. I am courageous and confident. I have more courage than I even know.

(Affirmations don't focus on the negative, because what you resist will persist, so focus on the positive).

Day 5- Low Self-Worth to Confidence

Take a few long slow breaths, feel everything relax.

Today is very important, because your whole life grows out of how you feel about yourself and reflects back to you.

It is never too late to strengthen in this area and turn it around.

Begin to dialog about self-worth. How is your self-esteem?

Explore any feelings and memories around what may have contributed to any low self-esteem. Write about anything or anyone that tore you down, or wore away at your feeling of self-worth. Whether it was an event or a season of your life, words that were spoken, etc.

Consider…(if you aren't sure where to start)

What do you think about yourself?

What are you insecure about?

Do you feel worthy?

Do you feel unsure about the decisions you make?

Do you struggle with low self-esteem?

How does this affect your life?

When you are done writing: be with your feelings, sit with it for a moment, accept what happened and let go of the hope it could have been any different.

If someone tore you down, consider what was their intention: to motivate you maybe? Was it coming from their fear base? Afraid you would not be successful or smart or thin or pretty or something superficial like that? Identify with them for a minute, how much pain or fear must they have been in, to project it onto you like that? Was that person given any encouragement or were they criticized too? Even if you aren't sure, allow that to release some of the sting of the event. Forgive yourself for contributing to low self-worth, self-abuse, or for not loving/encouraging yourself.

Forgive and release anyone who attacked you in any way and the pain of those events/attacks. In your own words…

Let it go, let it all go (you can get detailed if you want to).

Rebuilding

- Make a declaration to love, nurture and encourage yourself, and do your very best moving forward to ban any self-deprecating thoughts, or words any self-abuse of any kind, do your absolute best to not allow it any more. If you are someone that hates what you weigh, what you look like or anything else (superficial) about yourself, accept yourself right now exactly as you are. In your own words…I accept myself…

- Become your greatest encourager, this may take some practice; feel free to pat yourself on the back instead of waiting for someone else to do it.

- Own your space. You are here, you matter and you have been given life for a reason. Stand up tall you are worthy and you have a right to be here, life accepts you fully it's time to *fully* accept yourself.

- For the rest of this process declare: "I accept myself and approve of myself and I am worthy" for the next 30+ days, as many times a day as you can remember to. Say it out loud now a few times until it feels real.

- How are you confident? What areas of your life are you confident and sure about? Think of where your self-worth is healthy and strong. Can you translate those same beliefs to help you in areas that you have less confidence in?

Breathing exercise: Breathe in pure acceptance, fill up on it, and breathe out rejection of self, breathe in confidence- life accepts you fully. Exhale all thoughts of not being good enough, and breathe in self-acceptance and self-love. Do it for a few minutes and be with these new thoughts as you feel the shift.

Affirmations: I accept myself. I am confident. I approve of myself. I believe in myself. I am accepted. I am okay just the way I am. I have a right to be here. I am good. I am successful. I am smart. I am creative. I am unique. (Say these out loud, the harder an affirmation is to say the more work it needs, so repeat often- think of it like building a weak muscle).

Day 6- Abandonment to Connection

Welcome to day 6, great work so far. These are challenging "detox" days, but keep going- you are doing great.

Slow your breathing, deep easy breaths, allow your body and mind to relax and begin.

Today we are going to discuss any feelings of abandonment or loneliness. Is there anything painful you experienced regarding abandonment, whether physical, emotional or any other form of neglect?

Maybe you had a parent with an addiction, who wasn't there for you? Talk about it here, the pain that selfishness caused, etc. Give yourself a place to speak, hear yourself and connect, really let the anger and hurt have a voice. Go ahead and start writing.

Consider…(once you are done writing).

Do you have a fear of abandonment now?

Do you abandon others easily?

Are you guarded or extremely independent?

Are you lonely or have difficulty being alone?

Consider the parent or person that abandoned you, was it intentional? Were they dealing with their own pain and unable to give you what you needed? It wasn't because you were unlovable or did anything wrong, let yourself really feel and know that. It wasn't about you- they were incapable.

Are your ready to make peace with it and release the pain of the abandonment?

Forgive yourself for self-abandonment.

Forgive anyone that has ever abandoned you by *accepting* what happened- you do not have to agree with it.

Moving forward are you prepared to let down the walls and trust?

Are you willing to allow yourself the risk of being venerable and intimate?

Rebuilding

- In your own words: accept yourself back from your own abandonment, reconnect with yourself, and allow yourself to be open to self-intimacy.
- Loneliness can be amplified by an inability to be with yourself, and always looking to others to fill you up. Be open to a whole new relationship with you. You have the potential to be your best company: you have the same likes and dislikes, you enjoy the same things, you are fun and interesting and creative, so enjoy your own company.
- Have you let go of your hopes and dreams? Begin to allow yourself a voice again. Let your soul speak, what would it say, what does it really want?

Breathing exercise: Take some long slow deep breaths, inhale a new sense of connectedness, and exhale loneliness. Feel connection to self return with each breath as you fill up on it, connected and accepted.

Affirmations: I accept myself. I am enough. I am re-connected to myself. I am content and at peace. I am complete and whole. I love myself. Repeat often, affirm yourself more and more until it feels authentic.

Day 7- Shame to Freedom

Get comfortable, slow your breathing to deep easy breaths.

Today we are discussing shame and guilt.

Begin to think about any shame or guilt, is there anything you feel ashamed of, or guilty about? Any past behavior that caused shame, begin to let any feelings and thoughts about shame flow, and see what comes up. Think about anything you have done that created guilt or shame and get it out, no matter how embarrassing, silly, or crazy it was.

Consider...

Any actions that were a cry for help that you are now ashamed of?

Things you wish you could erase from your memory bank?

Feelings of guilt, that you weren't a better child, or teenager?

Feelings of guilt that you weren't a better parent?

Guilt or shame from cheating/unfaithfulness?

Shame you may be carrying from being a victim of abuse?

Release any shame and guilt of the past. Regardless of what you did or was done to you.

Shame or guilt can't serve you in your life, it has nothing to offer you anymore, so let it go. If you believe you need punishing for something you will punish yourself in some way (it can affect your health or limit success, etc.)

Therefore it is important to let yourself off the hook and forgive yourself.

In your own words: "I release shame and guilt from my past"...

Rebuilding (shame from abuse)

- Things can happen to us as kids that create a feeling of shame, that weren't our fault. If you were victimized, or abused as a child, it wasn't your fault, no matter what the perpetrator may have told you, you were an innocent child. It wasn't your fault. Now you say it: "what happened to me, wasn't my fault"...

- If you are haunted by any memories that remind you of traumatic events, can you associate something positive to that memory instead even if you have to make a new one? Overpower that memory with something good. Get a new image, even if it is imaginary (the brain doesn't know the difference) this may help ease the reaction any time you see something that triggers that memory.

- Refuse to keep playing that mental loop, resist the urge to go there, choose another thought, it may take some practice but you can get there. Shift to big picture thinking about your life instead of focusing on an event or a particular span of time. Don't give the perpetrator/abuser one more second of your life. Either way you get to choose how you spend the rest of your life- so don't give it all away in defeat.

- Accept what happened, give up the need to have it turn out any differently. Let go of the pain of it. It was what it was. It happened to you, it doesn't have to define you. It is not who you are.

Rebuilding (other guilt or shame)

- Part of life is figuring out who you are, how we do that is by trying all manner of different experiences, especially in our youth and 20's and beyond. Those experiences either helped to define us or let us know very quickly who we were not. Allow yourself the freedom to figure it out, no matter what age you are. Life is messy sometimes, it's not all neat and perfect and it's not supposed to be, part of the fun can be making a mess. Allow yourself the freedom to figure it out even if you make mistakes, without the shame and guilt.
- Don't put shame or guilt on others or use it to manipulate either or it will come back on you.
- When we know better-we do better, we don't have to feel ashamed if we didn't get it right somehow when we didn't know any better.

Activation: Imagine yourself standing at the edge of the Grand Canyon, wearing the jacket of shame/guilt you have been wearing all these years. Remove the jacket and hold it in your hands, feel the weight of it as you scrunch it up, then drop it over the edge of the canyon and tell it goodbye. Watch it drop down, and down until it is a tiny speck as it bursts into flames, the ashes disappear into the wind and the whole thing evaporates. It can never be worn by you again- it is gone.

Breathing exercise: Close your eyes and imagine inhaling innocence, contentment and peace and then exhaling shame and guilt, do that for a couple of minutes and fill up on peace and acceptance as any shame or guilt leaves your body and mind.

Affirmations: I am free. I am self-assured. I am fully accepted and confident. I trust myself. I am brave and courageous. I am good enough. I am proud of myself. I accept myself.

Day 8- Resentment to Acceptance

Welcome to day 8.

Take some deep breaths and get relaxed and comfortable to begin.

Today we look at regrets from the past as well as any bitterness or resentment.

This may be similar to other days covered so far, it is similar to the last one but it may bring up some different things for you that weren't covered on Day 7 (Guilt/Shame) or Day 2 (Sadness), but either way if you have an inner reaction to regret, bitterness or resentment, then talk it out- write about it here and face anything that comes up.

Accept what is because of decisions you made or that were made for you, all of it up to your current reality.

Consider…

Maybe you chose door A, instead of door B at some stage of your life and think that changed your whole direction for the worst?

Do you regret not working harder in school or picking different subjects or maybe another career path?

Resent being fired?

Bitter over a break-up or divorce?

Forgive yourself first of all, for any of the circumstances that hurt you either with regret, bitterness or resentment. Let yourself off the hook for any decisions you made or that were made for you. You are where you are, accept that regardless of where you wanted to be right now- accept where you are and trust life to improve as you grow and change.

Rebuilding

- Forgive yourself and trust your journey, you never know that decision you regret may actually be the best decision you ever made, you can't know for sure yet because you aren't at the end of the story.
- Find some positive things that came out of even a painful regret.
- Make the liberating decision to live with no regrets moving forward, even if you make a mistake in the future, you are still doing your best. Allow yourself the freedom of discovery and permission to step outside your comfort zone.
- Release yourself from any perfectionism. Constant regrets over even little things come from a fear based perfectionism that can create fear of failure and a need

26

to control. Let go of the need to have everything perfect and the constant pressure that comes with it.

- Have obtainable goals in your life, not expectations that are unachievable and leave you regretting what you didn't get done. Having a plan is good but also fluidity with it, to change the plan at any time if it isn't working for you.

Affirmations: I accept myself fully and completely. I believe and trust my decisions. I move forward with ease and confidence. I am at peace with my life.

Day 9-Unforgiveness to Forgiveness

Last day of Detox.

Get comfortable and relax, take a few deep breaths before you begin.

Today we are going to clean out any toxic feelings of un-forgiveness that may be still there. Is there anybody you have any animosity towards?

Maybe someone that came up yesterday while discussing resentment? Think about anybody you may need to forgive that has hurt you, whether it was someone that has been mentioned already in one of the other days or someone just coming to mind now? This may be someone from the past, recent years or even currently.

When their name comes up do you inwardly cringe? If so, that is probably a sign that you are still hanging on to some resentment that you need to let go of.

Write them a letter, you won't be sending it, so let it fly- this is your chance to vent. Let them know exactly how you felt, and how hurt you were by their actions.

The reason we aren't focusing on confronting the other person here is because the focus is on *your* freedom- we can't control someone else's reaction. I do believe we can get totally free without anyone else's agreement or validation. If you feel like you need/want to speak directly to someone that hurt you, I suggest doing this first and then checking in again to make sure you still feel it is the right thing to do. Accept what happened: see it for what it was.

Consider their perspective, did they mean to hurt you?

Considering what they did, have you done anything similar to anyone else at any time? If so, recognize we are more similar than we are different, and then let that go too.

Release the person that hurt you as best you can, forgive them and bless them on their journey so you can be free in yours.

In your own words…

If more than one person is coming up, write a letter to each one also (that you don't send). This will release negative emotional weight you don't need to be carrying around anymore, so make it a priority to get it done today or over the next few days (as soon as possible).

*

HEALING – Section 2

This next section is specific to healing the past: childhood/adolescence.
(Give your child-self a voice so they can stop screaming for attention
and validation).

Day 10- Child Voice (early memories)

Get comfortable and relax your whole body, take some deep slow breaths and begin.
Much of the reason we are stuck in our lives is because we are still hurting children that were never heard in our pain, we couldn't communicate then and often it comes out in our lives as adults. We are still subconsciously looking for comfort and acknowledgement.

Today we are going to use a visualization technique to help us.

Picture yourself as the spectator in the same room or space as you were as a child. Go back to your earliest negative memory when you weren't comforted or seen, heard or validated. What was happening, where were you as that little child?

Give yourself a moment to visualize the particular scene and go back there in your memory.

Now go to that child in their distress and comfort them, just like you would now if your child was crying.

Picture yourself picking them up or rocking them in a chair, hear their pain, connect and comfort the child, you will know what to say, it can be verbal or non-verbal communication. Rock them and comfort them as you acknowledge their pain, and bring them to a calm state.

Release the fear: let them know it wasn't their fault, and that they will be okay.

Don't worry if you don't remember all these points perfectly, the main thing is to hear the child in their pain and give your child-self the comfort they need.

Reassure them of their survival and your commitment to be there for them and with them.

Breathe and relax.

Good work.

Day 11- Child Voice (middle years)

Take some slow, easy breaths, and relax your whole body.
Today we are going to repeat the process from yesterday, but at a slightly older age.

Let your soul bring up to you another memory, as you arrive at another negative event that comes up.

Trust the process and repeat the healing outlined yesterday (Day 10).

Hear the child, comfort the child and validate them.

Maryanne Rodgers

Allow anything that needs to be healed come to your remembrance without pressure, give yourself time to connect to traumatic events and whatever needs acknowledging.

If your parents divorced in your childhood, spend some time there at that memory if that comes up.

Take your time: something will probably be triggered in your memory, let that be your guide. Repeat the process moving up through the childhood experience at different times of distress that stand out when you were not comforted, acknowledged or heard. Comfort that child as your adult self, now serving that distressed child. Hear the child, see the child and encourage the child. You will know what to say, either verbally or non-verbally. Hear, see and encourage the child, speak words of comfort and peace over the child, let them know that you know what they are/were going through.

You can stop at the teenage years or carry on through them if you want to (it's tomorrows assignment).

Breathe and relax.

Good work.

Day 12- Child Voice (teenage years)

Breathe deeply get still for a few moments and let your whole body relax.

Today we are going to repeat the process from yesterday this time as a teenager.

What were you feeling during your teenage years?

Your teenage self may speak the loudest, really let your teenage-self vent here, with all the ups and downs of that time you may have a lot to say and the teenager needs much encouragement.

Really hear the turmoil, whatever was not released at the time.

Many of us as teenagers didn't talk much or we didn't know how to articulate at the time, because it was such a struggling time.

Go there, go back there for a few minutes, your soul remembers how you felt in detail, so just be there for your teen-self and listen, let her/him know they matter and are significant.

Speak encouragement and hope to your teenage self: you will make it, it gets better, etc.

Feel yourself reconnect and as you accept your teen self, heard and validated.

Breathe and relax. Good work.

REPROGRAMMING - Section 3
This next section deals with subconscious beliefs that can limit us, constructed mostly in the early years of life.
What you believe will be your experience, change your belief and your experience will change.

Day 13- Core Beliefs: Identity/Individuality

Breathing slow and easy, get in a comfortable position and let your whole body relax (your shoulders, brow, even your teeth).

Go back in your memory and picture your family time as a child.

We all assumed roles in the family growing up, think about your place in the family. What was your identity- who were you in the family?

Dialog anything that comes up, give yourself a voice here.

Don't think too hard, say the first thing that comes to you...In my family I was...?

I was the...in the family?

Consider...

What did you learn about your place in the world from what you saw, heard and felt?

How did you need to behave in order to survive?

What traits did you take on to mask your personality?

Were you expected to do too much, lost in the shuffle of a big family or overly babied perhaps? Were you encouraged to be all you could be, or encouraged to stay average?

Were you accepted for who you really are?

When you are done writing or talking...

Accept it and make peace with it.

Those family years helped to shape you, either to let you know who you are or to make it clear who you are *not*.

Let go of any resentment you may still have....in your own words...

Release any false identity put on you by others.....in your own words...

Reprogramming

- Positive or negative treatment taught you about your perceived place in the world and shaped some of how you see yourself today. Your personality was already with you before birth, then came social conditioning that programmed you to fit into your family and the world around you. Do you know who you are without any self-limiting beliefs? With a little re-programming, your true identity can be re-discovered (or even discovered for the first time) as you become totally comfortable with who you are and fully embrace your individuality.

- Feel free to shed any mask and allow yourself to be more of who you really are and not just who you became to fit in. As you continue through this process you may begin to feel differently about your true self. Be free in your identity, maybe you aren't too sure about it, that's okay. Write yourself a new identity if you would like to, that feels more like you, or what you would like it to be.

- You are more than a single personality trait and a physical case, the real you is stronger and brighter than any label or limiting belief. You have a responsibility and a right to be who you truly are in absolute freedom.

Affirmations: I am free to be me. I am created perfectly. I accept my individuality. I accept myself fully and graciously. I embrace my true self. I am unique. I am a gift. I am always changing and growing. I have the power to be all I can be.

Day 14- Core Beliefs: Mothers/Women
Breathe and relax before you begin, make sure you are comfortable.
Today we look at what we learnt about mothers and women.
Think about what you learnt from your experience that became a subconscious core belief?
Mothers are…? Women are…?
Have a dialog here that is relevant to your experience, (what did you see, hear and feel)? Write or talk about what you learnt about mothers, her role in life and women in general.
Consider…
Were women/your mother respected in your family?
Were you raised by a single mother struggling to make ends meet?
Did you grow up to believe women could do anything with their life, or were you taught they should follow a preset gender role?
Do you have realistic expectations on women/mothers?
If you are a mother, are you different to your mother? How are you the same?
Are there areas that you don't/do want to repeat in your parenting style?
Are there things coming up here that you don't believe consciously now are true or correct?
Release anything that is no longer serving you…in your own words…

Reprogramming

- We are changing so rapidly with each generation, only a couple of generations back, women were locked into roles. Now women are very close to being totally free to choose (depending on culture) - but pretty amazing.
- Make peace with your experience and all that you learnt, whether it was freeing or limiting.
- Decide what you would like to believe today for your life, keep what works and let go or change what doesn't work for you. In today's society you get to negotiate your role in life much more, so design your life how you would like it to be.
- Forgive areas of weakness, if your mother disappointed you, abandoned you or wasn't there for you in a way you would have liked. Remember intention: was she doing the best she could, considering her own experience as a child? (She couldn't give you what she didn't have to give or what she didn't get in her childhood).
- Your mother may have completely failed you, if so maybe all you can say is "I survived!" Incredible, you made it anyway, that makes you strong and resourceful. Celebrate that and whatever else you can because of your experience.
- What is great about you because of your mother and her influence?
- Release your mother if you need to, release her as a woman and as your mother and bless her on her journey (even if she has passed on).

Day 15- Core Beliefs: Fathers/Men

Take a few deep relaxing breaths before you begin.
Today we discuss what we learnt about fathers and men when we were young?
What was your experience that formed your subconscious core belief about fathers and men?
Fathers are…? Men are…?

Have a dialog here that is relevant to your experience, write or talk about what you learnt about your father, his role and men in general. Consider...

Were men/fathers respected in your family?

Were you raised by a single father struggling to make ends meet?

Did you grow up to believe men had to follow a certain preset gender role?

Do you have realistic expectations on men because of your beliefs?

If you are a father, how are you different? How are you the same?

Are there areas that you don't/do want to repeat in your parenting style?

Are there things coming up here that you don't believe consciously are true or correct?

Release anything that is not serving you-any limiting belief...in your own words...

Reprogramming

- For those of us raised without fathers or with absent fathers, we can go looking for love in all the wrong places or the other extreme: try to avoid it altogether to minimize the risk of pain and disappointment. If you are living in either of these scenarios, it is possible to be healed as you keep talking it out, and make peace with the past. Relationships all carry risk, this is something you have to be willing to take when entering into any relationship. Being open to emotional intimacy, can be scary and risky especially if your own parents didn't let you know you mattered and were loved. But a life without intimacy that is a bigger loss. It's not too late if that is you and you are certainly not alone.

- For men, if you are fathers or will be fathers in the future how can you improve on your experience to not repeat the pattern? Or what about your father was good that you would like to imitate?

- Consider your fathers own experience with his father, how was his childhood? Was he capable of a close connection given his experience? Consider his intention: was he doing the best he could?

- If your father completely failed, and all you can say about it is: "I made it, I survived" then that is okay too. You did, so celebrate who you are because of (or regardless of) your experience.

- Forgive any disappointments from your father, face anything that comes up and let it go. Release him on his journey as a man and as your father and bless him to be all he can be (even if he has passed on).

Day 16- Core Belief: Children

Today we discuss what we learnt about children growing up that became a core belief? Have a dialog here that is relevant to your experience, write or talk about what you learnt from how children were treated in your experience.

Children are...?

Consider...

Were children valued in your family?

Were children loved unconditionally?

Tolerated or celebrated?

Were children spoilt with material possessions but not time?

Were they treated like an obstacle to free time?

To be seen and not heard?

Were children given a voice in your home?

How do you treat children now?

Did your experience contribute to your decision to have your own children?

Look at what came up, and face anything that is no longer serving you.

Let yourself grieve anything that was missing in your childhood, or for any bad treatment you had to face.

Forgive anyone that contributed to "messing up" your childhood. (Forgiveness is *acceptance*, not *agreement*).

Be at peace with your experience, come to peace with it and let go of any resentment or any limiting belief.

Reprogramming

- Most of us were raised by children themselves (in the last few generations: young adults were having kids in their late teens/early twenties) barely mature, and often repeating many of the same mistakes their parents made. This is a good place to be gracious to our parents and accept our experience, make peace with it if we need to. For most of us they probably did the best they could, with the emotional tools they had.

- If your childhood was a total nightmare and the best you can say is that you survived, then go with that. You are here, you made it, that is worth celebrating and now you probably have a profound message as well as compassion to help others who went through similar things.
- What was good about your childhood?
- What are you thankful for?
- How were you treated or recognized that you really appreciate?
- What about it made you stronger and the person you are today?

Day 17- Core Belief: Money

Welcome to day 17, you are doing great.

Here we discuss what we learnt about money that became a core belief?

Begin to think about your early experiences concerning money and what you were taught about it either verbally or non-verbally?

Money is…?

Consider…

What did your family think about money?

How did they handle money?

Were they open about money or very private?

Do you believe there is never enough, enough or plenty?

Do you have anxiety about money?

Are your beliefs about money serving you?

Would you like to change them?

In your own words…

Reprogramming

- If you come from a "lack mentality" you can change that, you don't have to have the same beliefs as your family or culture.
- Our experience becomes our belief, so if your experience teaches you that there is lack then that will be your experience. The key to a different experience is to start

to change your thinking about money if you need to. Every time you get money, bless it, every time you spend it bless it, bless your credit cards, even bless your bills. Blessing money might sound crazy but it will begin to change your relationship to money.

- Don't say things like: "I never have any money," "I am so broke" or anything like that or your experience will continue to line up with your words and you will continue to push money away. Change what you think, your words and how you act around money and you will begin to get a different experience.

- Begin to affirm plenty, even if you have to start with: I have enough for today! Start with what you can believe and go from there, and build as you go to affirming abundance until that begins to become your new belief, therefore changing your experience-changing your belief and making it easier to experience better.

- Be generous, let money flow out of your hands, so it can flow back in. Help people that have less than you, without judgment. Your act of kindness is what matters, what they do with your kind gesture is up to them, so give without conditions.

Affirmations: I have enough for today. There is plenty of money. I have everything I need. I have more than enough. I am generous. Money flows in and out of my life freely. I am wealthy.

Day 18-Core Belief: God/Spirituality/Religion
Take some relaxing slow easy breaths before you begin.
Today we discuss what we learnt about God, religion or spirituality? (When we were growing up).
Begin to open up and dialog about this, what did you learn from others about God during your impressionable years.
God is…?
Has that been your own personal experience since then?
In your own words…
Consider…
Were you taught to be afraid of an angry god?

Is your opinion of God based on what you have seen from man and religion?

How does, what you were taught (or not taught) effect your approach to spirituality now?

Do you have fear about making mistakes or not being good enough?

Can you decide who God is to you now without any pressure?

If your opinion of God based on what you have seen from man and religion, do you think that is accurate?

Reprogramming (freedom to choose)

- What you believe is absolutely up to you, if it is working for you- great, you may well be perfectly content with everything the way it is.

- I realize I am in dangerous territory here, as this is a passionate subject for many people. But since it's my book, here are my basic beliefs if anyone is interested: After more than 20 years of organized religion including what I consider a real connection/relationship with God; I kept the "relationship" and left the "religion." I now believe God is with all of us, and that there is no separation, just us forgetting that we are one with God and feeling/thinking we are separated. Anyone can have a spiritual experience (and an ongoing one if they want to) because when we reach out, God answers. He isn't so insecure that we have to do it an exact or precise way (He typically doesn't answer in an exact way all the time either). When your kids tug at your pants, and grunt up at you before they can speak or call you by any of 3 different names- that's your kid and so you respond. Same with God, except He *is* <u>unconditional love</u> without condition- try getting your head around that for a minute. Exactly, that's why people need religion to make it hard for themselves and others, for some reason we have a difficult time accepting unconditional love; we just can't seem to believe it could be that easy/good. Religion wore me out amongst other things, so now I keep it simple: unconditional love. Being good to others and not judging.

- Would you consider an experiment? Letting go of everything anyone else told you and simply be open to unconditional love. Let go of any preconceptions and fear and just *be*, without necessarily having to *do* anything. Can you accept unconditional love, free of any condition?
- Without any pressure, think about how you would like your spiritual life to be in your future or even in your wildest dreams.
- In your own words…you might like to write God a letter?

Affirmations: I am accepted by God. God loves me. I am safe. I can trust God. I am open to be loved by God. God loves me unconditionally. (Add your own if you would like).

Day 19-Core Belief: Relationships/Communicating

Welcome to day 19.

Today we discuss relationships and communication.

Think about what you learnt about relationships and communicating from what you saw and heard growing up.

Relationships are…?

Communicating is…?

Consider…

How did your family communicate?

Were they close, connected relationships in your family?

Did you get to communicate freely as a child or were you shut down?

Did you learn to scream or run (fight or flight) to cope with conflict?

If so, how has that affected your life?

In your own words…

Reprogramming

- Negative emotions often come up based on past experiences. We literally go back into our memory banks in a moment of conflict and find similar experiences, connect to the learned response and repeat the past patterns for the given situation. This can explain why a couple fights in the same exact way over an issue every time: one leaves and the other cries. They can't seem to push through the conflict and get to the

41

root issues, i.e.: one is feeling unloved and the other is feeling controlled. Or one is jealous and the other is defensive. Fear is the problem in all these scenarios, as fear usually reacts by attacking and the next thing you know you are fighting. What people in fear really need is reassurance, understanding and comfort. If you argue consistently about the same topic, suggest a distraction to your partner prior to the next time you get tempted to go down that road. One of you dance like a crazy person or shout out "purple crack monkeys" or put on a funny hat or something stupid to distract you. Any of these silly suggestions can work to break the unconscious rhythm you are stuck in. Anything that helps to break the intensity so you can calm down and get to the real issue. Find out what exactly is triggering you both and do your best to talk it out without accusation. I.e.: "when you …, I feel …"

- If you came from a chaotic environment with constant fighting, it probably feels somewhat comfortable and familiar for you, and peace can feel like the calm before the storm. Allow yourself to become more comfortable with peace and resist the urge to sabotage the calm environment.

- May I recommend meditation or yoga: it changes your mental chemistry and can turn anyone into a peaceful person. You can start very simply with a minute or two, (I don't sit in the exact posture), there aren't really rules you can do it how you want to, it's about getting still and connecting. Youtube does have some good basic demos you can watch, go to: youtube.com and type in: "meditation for beginners." You can also find Yoga on there.

Affirmations: I am a good communicator. I relate well to others. I am a calm partner and friend. I can talk to anyone about anything. I speak clearly and confidently. I am a clear and effective communicator.

Day 20- Core Belief: Work/Career/Purpose

Welcome to day 20, congratulations, you are halfway there!

Today we discuss what you learnt about work, and career?

Think about your core beliefs regarding work/career and decide if any belief is limiting you.

My work-life is…?

Consider…

Were you given room to pursue your natural talents and passions?

Were you raised believing that you have a purpose or a calling?

What do you believe about that now?

What do you believe about career or work-life now?

Did you follow in anyone's footsteps out of duty?

Did you challenge the family story in some way?

Do you believe in making enough money to survive or is doing what you love more important to you?

Are you happy as long as you have a job and can support your family?

In your own words…

Reprogramming

- First of all, it's important to know who you are, and why you are here, before you can decide what to do with your life. Essentially we are all here to help, to heal, to give, to add to the collective somehow, no matter what you do for a living, do your best to serve others. If you find what you do now to be soul-destroying, then find something else to do.

- Finding the right livelihood is one of the most important components in your life since you spend most of your time working it is vital to at least like it and hopefully bring your best self to what you do.

- What would you do with your days if money was not a factor at all (if you had unlimited funds). Think about how your life would be- say after the first couple of years traveling the world and life got back to normal, how would you spend your days? What would a typical day look like? Where would you find the most joy? Can you have that in your life now?

- Write a list of all your favorite experiences, things, sights, sounds, environments when you feel most alive what are you doing, feeling? Add to this list over the next few days. (We will refer back to your list on another day also)

Word list example: sun, travel, people, sewing, laughter, rest, ocean, helping, peaceful, baseball, happy, children, running, affection, painting, winning, light.

Affirmations: I am open to my right livelihood. I move forward with ease. I bring light to everything I do. I have many talents. I can do anything I choose to do. I love to serve others. I work with a good attitude. I put love into what I do. I meet the right people at the right time.

Day 21-Core Belief: Sex/Intimacy

Welcome to day 21 (you might want to do some breathing before this one).

Today we are going to discuss sex and intimacy(in-to-me-see).

What did you learn about sex growing up?

What are your beliefs about it now?

Sex is...?

Consider...

Was sex discussed openly, privately or not at all?

Were the correct names used for body parts: penis and vagina?

Do you consider yourself a sexual person?

Do you have any hang-ups that hinder you in a sexual/intimate relationship?

In your own words...

Reprogramming

- There is still a lot of shame and embarrassment about sex even in our overly sexed culture. It is still a new thought to be open about enjoying sex. Sex is a gift for us to enjoy, not to be abused or misused, and not so fun or fulfilling without love.

- Most of us weren't told a whole lot about sex (unless you consider a 5 minute chat in-depth) so we figured it out and pieced together information from the playground sometimes quite literally. Are you open to getting more educated about sex or learning some new moves? Would you buy or borrow a book that you wouldn't normally read on the subject? Don't feel like you have

to put on a chicken suit and swing from the ceiling –
there are lots of ways to have fun, it just takes a little
imagination.

- If you don't usually initiate sex with your partner, think
of an interesting way to get things started, i.e.: a
different time of day or somewhere different (just don't
get arrested). If you usually initiate, try hanging back
and give your partner a chance to. After a week- or
three, assume initiation role and I apologize for the
suggestion ☺.
- Guys: the more romance you give a woman the more sex
you will probably get in return 99.9% of the time. Small
gestures go a long way.
- Gals: we shut a man down sexually by belittling him and
putting him down, instead encourage and admire him-
if you want some that is.
- Have fun~!

Affirmations: it is good to enjoy sex. I am free to enjoy my body. I
am a sexual being. Sex is fun. Sex is part of life. Sex is normal and
healthy. I like/love having sex/making love.

Day 22-Core Belief: Judgment/Criticism

Take some slow deep easy breaths and relax before beginning ...
Today we discuss judging and criticizing others?
What did you learn about judging and criticizing others? What did you
learn about judging and criticizing yourself?
Dialog about this and decide if anything is limiting you now?
In your own words...
Consider...
Do you find yourself judging all the time?
Are you critical of other people's choices in life?
Do you judge someone because they are homeless *or* drive a Ferrari?
Do you judge when you are jealous?
Do you judge when you think you are better?
Reprogramming

- Be aware of the inner critic, by trying a judgment free
day; one day without deciding what you or someone
else does, how they look/how they dress or what they

say is wrong. It's quite liberating, and the less you judge others the less you will judge yourself.

For one day, try observing life without judgment.

- Next time someone does something that bothers you but doesn't directly affect you, sit with it and try and figure out why it is bothering you so much- how does it relate to your past? There may well be a connection and that is why it irritates you.
- How boring would life be if we were all an exact clone of each other? Celebrate our differences by accepting others and not feeling the need to decide if they are right or wrong. "Different" is not necessarily wrong. It is just another way.
- I believe we can do better than tolerance, tolerance might stop me from killing you, but it is far from acceptance. Acceptance doesn't mean we have to agree, but we can accept others no matter what.
- Being critical can be a hard habit to break and can have you literally obsessing about what is wrong all the time. Lighten up on your children and spouse if you do this often, let your eyes light up when you see them- let them know you are happy to see them, don't always be looking for what is wrong with their appearance and picking at them or they could become insecure people-pleasers.
- Find a glass jar or container and give yourself a "fine jar" and fine yourself to keep yourself in check, whenever you judge or criticize someone. You will quickly zip-it when it costs you something. (This idea can also work for any other bad habit).
- Anytime you attack or criticize another, you are literally shooting yourself in the foot, it will come back somehow someway so save yourself the pain.

Affirmations: I accept all. I accept the differences that make us all unique. I am gracious towards others. I see and appreciate the beauty in our differences. I encourage liberation and freedom. I release others from my expectations.

Day 23-Core Belief: Prejudice

Welcome to day 23, we are almost through this section- great work!
Today we discuss what we learnt about discrimination or equality based on differences/prejudices: race, sexuality, politics, religion, etc.?
People that are different to me are...?
Begin to dialog here and get honest about any subtle beliefs that come up.
In your own words...
Consider...
Do you have prejudices? Do you pre-judge people?
How do you respond to people with different lifestyles or beliefs to you?
Do you think you are superior to others because of your race, religion, age, looks, income, title or possessions?

Reprogramming

- We have many of the things we have simply because we were born into a certain family, country, class, and status, which we had zero control over. Imagine you were born in a different country, to another family, class and economic status. Your whole life would be different: you would look different, think differently and act differently with more or less choices. Check yourself on your tolerance levels, we are all the same- none better, none worse- equal. What separates us is only 0.1% of our DNA (how we look).

- Do you treat people better based on how they look, or their age? Immaturity only wants to relate to an identical demographic. Next time you are at a gathering, talk to someone outside of your age and stage in life and you may be surprised how interesting they are. Older people can be fascinating and a lesson in life (either how to be *or* how not to be), they have seen more days, and usually have pearls of wisdom to share if we will listen.

Affirmations: (can you come up with a couple of good ones here)?

BIG PICTURE - Section 4

In this next section, we step back and look at things with a little perspective.

Day 24- Owning It

Today we are going to look at accepting responsibility for our lives. Feel free to talk about it here (is there anything blocking you from taking responsibility)?

Many of us secretly or subconsciously blame others, it is a lot easier to do, taking responsibility is not, but it's a good time in this process to own our life completely.

- Owning it, actually gives you your life back instead of blaming any/everybody else. Taking responsibility simply means no matter what happened to you in the past, letting go of the hope that it could have been any other way and accepting where you are right now. Then moving forward empowered as the captain of your own soul, and no longer a victim.

- If you are having a problem with a co-worker or relative, take responsibility for your part. What is the trait in them that is irritating you? Is it showing up to show you to yourself? Consider: how do you demonstrate the same thing (maybe in a different way). Are you both showing fear? (One is controlling and the other is defensive? Think it through alone first, own your part of it and then approach it carefully and sensitively if need be with the person you are having the issue with.

- You are also responsible for your moods and the energy you carry. That energy causes people to either be moving towards you or away from you. Are people drawn to you or leaving your life? The more you settle these inner issues, the more you can radiate light and attract everything you want into your life, including the right people. When there is an energy shift, the wrong people will either start to leave your life or not be who you feel like being around any longer. We are magnets either attracting or repelling there is not much neutrality –it is a powerful universe we live in. When people leave your presence they should feel better not worse, so choose every day to bring the light.

Blackboard technique

(I use this as a way for my soul/subconscious to communicate to me, it's just a way of tuning in to anything I may be missing on a conscious level). You can try this to see if you still have an emotional charge when you think about blaming anyone else for your life.

Get really still for a few moments.

Close your eyes and imagine you are looking at a big blackboard in your mind. Think about who is responsible for your life being the way it is- does anyone come up when you think about that? Watch and see if a name or face comes up, whatever you get. Give yourself a moment to understand and see the connection. Now take a big eraser and wipe that image or name off the board and with it all negative energy and feelings attached, see it also leaving your mind and body. Then write your name on the board (in big bold letters). Accept accountability moving forward for your life without pressure and with complete peace for the future.

Affirmations: I accept my life. I take complete ownership for my life. I am responsible for my life moving forward. I move forward with ease. Life is kind to me.

Day 25- Embracing the Journey

Welcome to day 25.

Today is similar to yesterday, but today we embrace our journey and future.

Think of all your experiences throughout your life and how they have helped to make you all the incredible qualities you are today.

What from your history has made you who you are today?

Having survived certain things, may mean you are able to take care of yourself for example. Embrace your path and your journey so far and shift into hope for the future.

Think about how many people you can help or relate to, because of your journey?

Who do you have compassion for?

What moves you?

Look at what you are thinking today…are these thoughts going to create the kind of life you want to create?

Look at what you are saying…is that how you wish to frame your world?

Look at your actions…are they the best expression of who you are?

See these things as bricks stacking together to build your life, if your bricks were made of a certain material what would they be made out of? Gold, rock or crappy dirt? See yourself as the builder, selecting the material every day that comes together to create what you live in tomorrow…so choose wisely.

You can create a completely new and different life if you would like, you just have to send out the messages you want to come back. I am repeating myself for a reason.

Never say: "my life is a mess" or "I hate my life" or "I don't have a future" or anything like that or you will add fuel to that same fire. Start a fire of abundance and joy, feed that fire instead, throw some logs on that fire! Stoke the fire, be willing to put a little effort in to keep it going. Don't feed the fire of doubt and defeat.

The good, the not so good, the hills and valleys, all become part of your life collage and it will be a thing of beauty one day when you stand back and see it from the right perspective, maybe even a masterpiece.

Blackboard technique

You can use the blackboard technique again here if you like. (It could be a billboard, a whiteboard or a blank canvas- if you prefer). I call it a blackboard, but it doesn't matter- it's about creating a space to connect. So imagine you are looking at a large board (close your eyes). When you think about your future, what comes up on the board? Allow what wants to come up. Are there any negative or fearful images, words or feelings coming up? When they stop, take out your big eraser and clean the board until all the old negative words, patterns, fears, low expectations, are gone.

Now think about your future- it should feel more neutral.

Then let new words, images, and feelings come up, creating a new beautiful picture of your future, sit with that as you settle into new hopeful images.

Affirmations: I bless my journey. I am on the right track. I like my life. My life is moving in the right direction. Everything I need is coming to me. I see the perfection in my life. I embrace my life. My future is bright. My future is safe. I love my life.

Day 26-Inspiring Pictures

Today we are creating new pictures for your life that will help to strengthen positive emotions.

Imagine your ideal life...

What does it look like? But more importantly- what does it feel like? We all want a better life, and we all want to feel as good as we possibly can.

Today's assignment is to create a "Feel Good Board" typically called a "Vision Board," but with a slight twist. Instead of pictures of the perfect house, or car or some hot model, try and find pictures that are more intangible that create the feelings you would like.

Cut out and collect pictures (from magazines, old books, or print from the Internet) that *feel* good to you: images of happiness, peace, or pleasure, from different colors, words or pictures- anything that makes you feel good. You can put this together in a scrap book or on a poster board. It works well if you put it somewhere you can easily see it, but if you prefer to have it be something private then opt for a journal or scrap book. Then when you look at the pictures, connect with those feelings and imagine your life feeling that good. See your life moving towards that and do your part to re-enforce those feelings with good thoughts.

Why am I suggesting this? Because as you create good feelings, no matter where they come from (even from a 1 dimensional picture) it makes you feel good and can help your brain to produce serotonin, the "feel good" hormone. More lasting is the fact that as you become strategic in your thought selection, your life will start to take on a new life of its own and adjust itself in constructive ways to fit your new frequency. Amazing things start to happen, for the very reason you are making clear requests. Creativity can come alive, new ideas start to flow and miracles made way for.

If you don't know what you want, how can life bring you the right thing? So get clear about what you want, as your beliefs line up with these affirming images and thoughts. Every day, look at your pictures and say "thank you." Move into and declare yourself to have those feelings by choice every day. "I feel good today, I feel happy"- tell your brain what it will be, tell it to be happy and it will be. Maybe not the first time you say it, but by the 5th you will start to feel a shift.

If you aren't up for doing one of these boards, that's okay, (you could paint a picture or use your word list from Day 20). The point is to have a picture of where you see yourself, how your life will look and feel down the road, because that creates your future. So pick healthy, happy, positive, hopeful images because consciously or unconsciously you will head towards your choices.

Every day look at the board say "thank you" as though you have already received it and move into those feelings.

Affirmations: My future is bright. I expect good always. My future is full of happiness. I feel good about my future. I trust life. My life gets better and better. Everything is working for my benefit.

Day 27 –Livelihood
Welcome to day 27- great work so far!
Take some good deep breaths and begin…
Today we explore finding the right livelihood, lifework, career, etc.
If this is an important subject for you, you may want to break it into a couple of days or skip through it if you are completely satisfied in this area.
Do you like what you spend most of your days doing?
How does what you do make you feel about who you are? Is it a true reflection of the best possible you?
If it is- great, maybe for some just a couple of adjustments would make it ideal? Where you do it, or how you do it, may change the whole thing for the better for you?
If you are content to have a job with benefits then that is fine too.
Maybe your career is raising your kids, very important work and if so, hopefully you see the tremendous value in that?
If you choose to believe you can truly love what you do and be excited about your life/ work, then also remain open to *how* you could do that.
Go back to the word list you wrote on Day 20 (Core belief: Career)
What do you have on your list that is *being*? (Peaceful, happy, helping/helpful, rest/restful, even the word "people" could mean: connected, companion, friendly, heard, caring etc. Look for the *being* on your list, and find your feeling state: i.e., sun- gives me a feeling of warmth and comfort *being* warm and comforted, calm and happy. Now also with your *doing* words- recognize the feelings you get from *doing* whatever it is.
What we really want in life is the feelings that doing these things bring.

You can simply *be* the list (feeling states) regardless of what you are *doing* for work and in the process your *doing* may change almost on its own.

Daily tasks are irrelevant if you are *being* your true and best self.

Can you *be* it now? Can you act as if you love what you do, because you get to *be* you? And see if you don't begin to move naturally towards a more custom fit livelihood.

Rebuilding (clarity will come)

- Discover and decide who you are and be that, no matter what, everywhere you go, be that without force or effort, it should be effortless: teacher, healer, caregiver, listener, giver, inspirer, deliverer, peacemaker, repairer, mentor, director, counselor, coach, motivator, mediator, encourager, cheerleader, protector, trainer, lifter, designer, assistant, aide, illuminator, lover, creator, inventor, intuitive. Who do you find yourself *being* mostly? If you connect to "teacher" you don't have to take it literally by deciding to be a teacher in a classroom necessarily, it might come to you in a completely new or different way (while still being a teacher).

- Our greatest joy comes from bringing who we are into the space and *adding* to somehow, true calling is wrapped up in contributing to the collective. The *how* is not so important. Whether, you sell, clean, sing, serve, or write. Bring the light, be the light, be the love, the joy, the hope, the laughter, the peace, the acceptance, when you are being your authentic self, you will bring it.

- Don't worry about figuring out "*how*" you can get to a more fulfilling career. Focus on what makes you happy and more of yourself, what comes easily to you and helps others. The *how* will begin to reveal itself, just be open, listen and trust your gut (not your head trying to figure it out) it will most likely come as a whisper, an inspiration or maybe you will meet the right person at the right time.

Affirmations: I am open to the right path. The right livelihood is being made known to me. I am open to what makes me happy. I bring the light to everything I do. I embrace who I really am. I love what I do. I love to help others.

Day 28-Your People

Welcome to day 28.

List anyone you can think of that has ever believed in you, encouraged you or loved you, they can be anyone living or passed (alive in spirit). You can list them in groups if that is easier: family, people from your company, school, church, etc.

Think about that list and add to it whenever you think of someone else. These are all the people that believe in you and are cheering you on in life.

Imagine taking this cheer team with you wherever you go, remember them anytime you need a confidence boost or a little encouragement. We are all connected, you technically aren't alone if you really think about it. You have people standing with you whether you remember them or not, see them or not and that doesn't even count your angels.

Activation: Feel that love for a minute, imagine every face that ever believed in you, like a big patchwork quilt of love woven together to create a large blanket wrapped around you. Put that blanket on anytime you need to remember you are loved. (You can use a real blanket and imagine all these people) this can actually help to boost the production of the "cuddle hormone" Oxytocin)

Affirmations: I am loved. Many people believe in me. I matter. I am important. I am part of the collective family. I feel encouraged. I am wrapped in love. I am comforted.

Day 29-Like Family

Today we are celebrating people that have been like family to us, though they aren't necessarily related by blood. Sometimes we forget how many people have been placed around us to bless us and help us on our journey.

This can be particularly significant if you only had one parent, were raised by other relatives, in foster care or had a splintered family etc. Think of how many great people you have been blessed with: mentors, role models or people you felt were *like* a parent to you, *like* a grandparent, or *like* a sister, brother, uncle or aunt? Who has been or is like a mother? Who has been or is like a father to you?

Appreciate them, and let them know how awesome they are in your life: reach out somehow if you want to.

Also consider who is younger than you that you could mentor, inspire or encourage in some way?

Affirmations: I am part of a family. I am loved. I am surrounded by people that love me. I am precious. I matter to many people.

SELF-CARE - Section 5
Taking care of the VIP in your life- you.
To the level you love yourself is the level you will be loved.

Day 30- Personality

Today we are going to look at all the wonderful facets that make up your personality, embracing and accepting the whole package.

Make a list of all your positive personality traits, and then come back.

We all have a couple of annoying personality traits or areas we are still working on. So next, objectively list negative personality traits also, don't go crazy on yourself and list everything known to man.

Then, when you are done with that list, next to each negative trait: write why having that trait is also positive.

Examples:

Interrupt= *Passionate*

Hypersensitive= *Insightful and Creative.*

Now add each *new* positive to the first list of positive personality traits that you wrote. Then erase or draw a line through the negative list.

Accept yourself- the total package, as you realize there is a pro to every con. Accepting that the work of art- you, isn't quite complete yet.

Embrace it all, and accept your total self, with strengths and weaknesses. Let there be a peace and a neutrality about all that makes you-you.

This might be a good place for a breathing exercise...

Focus on your breath for a moment, then breathe in, inhaling acceptance and grace, and exhaling any disapproval, judgment or self-judgment you may still have. Repeat for a few minutes until you feel a shift to a relaxed peace and total acceptance.

Affirmations: I embrace my total self. I accept me. I like me. I am an original. There is no one quite like me. I am a compilation of wonderful gifts. (Feel free to add a couple of good ones here too).

Day 31-Self Soothing

Welcome to day 31.

Get nice and comfortable, take some relaxing cleansing breaths and begin.

How do you self-sooth?

What is your main pacifier of choice or maybe you have a few?

Consider...

What do you do when you are stressed/anxious?

What do you do when you are angry?

What do you do when you feel lonely?

What do you do when you feel down?

What do you do when you are happy?

Is your typical self-soothing something that is hindering or hurting you? Does it create a negative cycle in your life?

Rebuilding

- Do you have enough soul feeding activities in your life? What else could you do that you really enjoy? Have you given up doing something you really like that you could pick up again?

- Are you prepared to consider something else that may be more beneficial? I.e.: Instead of eating a tub of ice cream and then beating yourself up the next morning you could try…? When you feel…? Be real here, find something you could realistically exchange, or even something similar, but a better option (like sorbet instead of ice cream, 2 scoops instead of 6).

- Is there a day or time of day you don't particularly like? How can you switch it up? If you don't like Monday mornings, maybe you could wear your favorite outfit and allow yourself your favorite breakfast that day? Or meet a friend for coffee before work? If you don't enjoy Saturday nights at home alone with the TV, can you have a standing date with a friend where you walk or workout together, or go to different ethnic food restaurants every week? Join a social club, a singles club, a poker game, or visit a fun/interesting relative?

- Change it up- mix it up, re-arrange your life, you are the architect and composer, you pick the music and the colors, so make it want you want. I know there are plenty of excuses and reasons why you can't: "the kids," or "limited funds" but don't let your imagination and creativity die just because you might have a few limitations logistically right now. Build a fort in the front room with the kids, have a game night, or a creative art night with whatever you can find.
  Turn off the electronics and connect somehow.

Blackboard technique

You can use this technique anytime something is bothering you- or if you need help recognizing what is bothering you or why you want to self-sooth in a particular way.

Picture your blackboard, think about whatever it is that is bothering you, or think about self-soothing. Then watch to see what words, images or feelings come up on the blackboard in your mind, watch as they pop up one by one, (or it might only be one). What is bothering you, what words or images are coming up? Do you see a connection? It may be to something from the past. Take out your big eraser and clean the board until it is all gone- clearing the negative energy from your life. Then allow new words, feelings and images to come up, that bring you greater comfort than your self-soothing would have. Nestle into that peace and let feelings of safety and contentment wash over you. **Affirmations**: I am complete. I am enough. I am worthy. I matter. I have what I need. I am loved. I am strong. I am comforted. I am connected to myself. I am safe.

Day 32- Best Environment

Look around you, does your space make you feel good?

Today is about creating the best possible environment, and to think about the space you live in, not just visually.

How is the atmosphere in your home?

What if anything would you like to do to improve it?

Does your world reflect who you are?

Is it clean and tidy, attractive and inspiring?

Peaceful and safe emotionally?

Is it the very best you can afford yourself?

Are your spaces (car, house, workspace) pleasant places to be?

How do they make you feel?

Maybe the first step is a really good clean and some organization, that alone could improve how you feel.

You could create a space in your home that is especially for you to relax and renew yourself, even if you live alone.

Make your world as beautiful as you can, clean, tidy and attractive- for you first as well as everybody else.

How do you want people to feel when they are in your space? Does it say what you want it to?

Consider color, lighting, textures (an assortment), good dimensions, flow and accessories (clutter can make people feel tense or trapped). A few well-chosen items may be all you need.

Make notes about any ideas you have or changes you would like to implement while we are discussing this today.

Rebuilding (creating harmony)

- Come up with your own ideas for anything you might like to change or improve. Here are some of mine...
    - You could paint a feature wall or a room? It's very easy and inexpensive and if you don't like it, you can always paint it back. All you need is newspaper or old blankets to cover the floor/furniture, painters tape, a brush, a roller, base paint and paint color of choice. You can buy a small sample before you commit and try it on the wall first. (If you need step by step directions you can go to: youtube.com for video demonstrations).
    - Changing cushions, an area rug or pictures can make a big difference also and doesn't have to cost a lot.
    - Candles and soft lighting can really cozy-up a room, change any bright light bulbs to create a softer environment.
    - Buy or pick flowers for yourself to brighten your space.
    - Put up pictures or quotes that inspire you.
    - Change the feel by rearranging the furniture.

Rebuilding (atmosphere)

- Put out a "fine jar," or a chore list for anyone disturbing your environment (fighting, name calling, swearing or whatever else you want *out* of your environment) as a motivational tool. Or you could do a reward system for *not* doing it- whatever works best specific to your family.
- It's your house, you get to decide what you do or don't want in it. Some people have a rule, they check their attitudes at the door, no bringing work stress home, or walking in pissed off. Whatever adds peace to your environment, at least something to be aware of.
    I used to know a woman that blasted her husband with a to-do-list the minute he walked in the door, amazing he even came home. Nagging- so *not* sexy.

Day 33-Self Love/Self Talk

Today we are discussing self-talk, though hopefully by now in the process, as more of a refresher.

How would you say the self-dialog is since starting this process? Improved? It can take a while, especially if you have been beating yourself up for years. Stay with it, do your best to remove all needless pressure and speak more kindly and accepting.

Take your own inventory here, and consider any improvements you would like to make, not just in how you speak to yourself but how you take care of yourself in general?

Do you agree to do things you really don't want to do, but find yourself unable to say no? Are you a "people-pleaser" that puts your own needs at the bottom of the list? If this is you- practice saying "no" over the next few days. There are kind ways to say it: "maybe next time," "that's not really my thing," "sounds tempting but I will have to pass, thanks anyway though."

Rebuilding

- Wouldn't it be great to get encouragement from yourself instead of needing it from others? We are so used to looking for everything we need emotionally to come from someone or somewhere else, but what if we could give ourselves anything we need emotionally- I truly believe it is possible to get to that place. I challenge you to try it, next time you have an emotional need- be that for yourself. (I am not saying that we don't need anyone but it should be more of a bonus than out of desperation).

- How you are doing on the subject of "taking care of yourself." Do you eat well? (Not just staying thin to attract a mate, but out of self-care and love). Do you feed your soul doing a recreational activity that makes you feel good? Are you physically active? (Not just to look attractive to others, but for your own health and vitality). Is there something you enjoy doing that is physical at the same time?

- Do you sit quietly with yourself and connect somehow? Do you meditate, journal or get creative in some way that centers you and creates a sense of peace and connection? (You could start with just 1 minute per day meditating; sit there close your eyes and focus on the miracle of your breath, on unconditional love, or just smile and relax).

- Take your left hand and wrap it around your right shoulder, then take your right hand and place it on your left shoulder and squeeze tight, yes that is a hug. Available on demand.

Blackboard technique
Let's use this technique here to see if there are any blockages or hindrances in this area or any connections to the past still holding you in a negative pattern. Close your eyes and see the blackboard in your mind. Think about taking care of yourself, then watch any words, or images (you might get a feeling instead) come up on the blackboard, let whatever wants to come up appear on the board. Observe any feelings and associations from the past. Then take out your big eraser and clean the board until all the negative connections are gone. Now allow new words and feelings to come up, sit with those and get a new picture of acceptance, unconditional love and safety (whatever comes to you).
Affirmations: I take care of myself. I accept myself. I am good to myself. I matter. I am worthy of love. I am comfortable with myself. I love me. I like me.

Day 34-Date Night!
Welcome to day 34, great work so far.
I thought we would have some fun, today is all about planning a date with yourself. Yes I'm completely serious. ☺
How comfortable are you with this idea?
Have a think about what kind of date you might like to make it, without any pressure. I'm sure there are a lot of things you can think of, but regardless of what you do, this is a great way to *be* with yourself. Carve out some time that will work, (the more time the better) preferably over the next few days if you can.
Today we are planning it out. So decide on the *when*, put it on your calendar and do your very best to stick to it. Even if some "hottie" calls, they can wait a day, just tell them you have "plans."
This takes a mental shift to purposely plan a special time for *yourself.*
You get to pick the movie, the food, your outfit, the shopping, the beach/lake, the time, the day whatever you like!
Is there something you have wanted to do, but haven't had the chance yet, or maybe a little shopping for something special?
Take yourself somewhere or do something you would really enjoy and stay engaged and connected, treat yourself as a special VIP.

Treat yourself with kindness and respect like you would on any other important date. You might just have a great time!
Affirmations: I am good company. I am fun. I like spending time with myself. I am great company. I have much to contribute. I am loving and kind to myself. I am loving towards others.

Day 35- Love Letter

Have you ever written a love letter?

Today we are going to write a love letter to ourselves.

Yippee! Oh come on- it's not that bad. Good for you.

If that is too big a stretch, start with a like letter and work towards a love letter. If this is icky and uncomfortable for you, then it's a good sign this is going to be a good exercise and a new perspective. (A good thing to do before your date assuming you haven't gone on it yet).

In your own words…let it flow- it doesn't have to be perfect.

This is healthy, I know it sounds weird, but it's unfortunate how hard it is to be nice to ourselves let alone love ourselves.

Continue to commit to not put yourself down at the very least and at the very best- go ahead and fall in love with yourself (we expect or at least hope another to, so why can't we)?

No more looking in the mirror attacks, instead, look at your best asset and tell yourself how great you are. As the inside is beautifying and being more accepted, that will show on the outside. Keep this letter somewhere you keep other important items and read it anytime you need encouragement or to reconnect.

Get writing, you will be glade you did ☺

Maryanne Rodgers

CELEBRATE LIFE –Section 6
Finishing touches-putting it all together, creating joy moving forward.
Decide your life will be beautiful and it will be so.

Day 36-Thankful

Today we look at everything in our lives right now that is working, all that is good and for how much we can be thankful for.

Are you naturally thankful? I'm not sure many people are thankful naturally. We have to teach kids to be thankful. We didn't come in to the world particularly thankful did we-Waaaa!

It is never too late to become a thankful person, it will change your days and ultimately your life. Thankfulness immediately shifts our perspective to what is going right instead of looking at what is wrong all the time. Ego has to take a back seat when we are thankful, because the ego is never satisfied, so the very act of gratitude itself silences our ego and gets us out of that driving need to acquire things all the time. A good habit is to name a few things you are thankful for every day, feel free to mix it up. Being thankful, will give you more things to be thankful for- shifting your perspective. Just like complaining gives you more things to complain about.

Reminds me of a funny story: I was with a friend a few months ago in Las Vegas, she went off on the hotel receptionist about our room after a long and exhausting flight. There was something wrong with her lunch and with every situation after that- something to complain about. By the time it had happened for about the third time (her drink had a hair in it) we looked at each other and laughed as we realized what was happening. Boy- that day was a live lesson in how the energy we create reproduces itself, (either negative or positive) and can very quickly comes back at us in the same way.

Create positive energy by being thankful every day, giving yourself more to be thankful for as the obedient Universe repays you in kind. Be thankful every day, for your life, your future and everything in between. Remember to be thankful for intangibles also (things you can't see) and for things you have never had to live without, that most of the world do, i.e.: running water, or plumbing.

Write down or say 5 things you are thankful for today and consider making it a regular habit.

Affirmations: I am a thankful person. I have much to be thankful for. I see good in everyone. I appreciate life and all it contains. I am full of gratitude. I am thankful for unconditional love.

Day 37- Creating Conscious Days

How do you start your day?

Do you wake up worried or complaining about all the things you have to do? Changing your mornings or how you start your day can absolutely change your life. "Clearing your head" is the trick.

Some great ways to do that are: exercise, meditation or journaling. Meditating for just 15 minutes in the morning (at night too if you can) makes a huge difference to your day. For some people this sounds as foreign as learning another language but at least try it once and see if you don't feel more peaceful, aware and connected. Start with a minute or two if that is easier and just focus on your breathing (keep it simple). Maybe you would prefer to exercise, either activity lifts your energy in a positive way.

Many people journal at the end of the day, but may I suggest in the beginning of the day, as one of the first things you do. It has an effective way of clearing out all that mental chatter before the day gets going. This type of journaling is without guidelines, it doesn't even have to make sense, just write whatever comes to you and keep going until you feel mentally clear (an inexpensive notebook is all you need). Answers can come to you miraculously while doing this cleansing practice, try it just once and see if your day isn't brighter and lighter than usual. I highly recommend it especially if you are pursuing more creativity in your life.

Other suggestions: stretching, walking, running, yoga, kick boxing, dance, prayer, reading (non-fiction), writing affirmations, quotes, music (or a combo of the selection if time permits). Find what works best for you and switch it up or try something else every now and again if you prefer variety. I.e.: put on some relaxing music, write as the coffee is brewing, then do some stretches and mediate for a few minutes (it doesn't have to be hours).

The harder getting into this space in the morning is, the more it will probably benefit you. Treat the first hour of the day as sacred if you possibly can, even if that means getting up before everyone else in the house. It will change your day and be worth the sacrifice.

If you stub your toe getting out of bed, get back into bed, once the pain subsides, laugh and try starting it over again before you decide "this is going to be a bad day." You get to decide, life is not happening to you- you are creating it.

Once you get used to starting your day in a more connected way, you will be more consciously aware and unsettled by stress or drama.

Creating joy...

The occasional dance mix helps elevate energy levels in a more direct way. Before leaving the house, try some disco, my favorite old 70's song is: "Carwash" it really gets you pumped- try having a bad day after boogying around the kitchen to Carwash!

Yes these are the extremes I go to, (especially when I was facing a potentially stressful day at work) and it works!

Use your commute as an encouraging mental environment, coach yourself and declare it to be a great day. You are literally creating your day in those first few minutes and hours, it's a blank canvas so make it what you want it to be and set the tone for the day.

Creating peace...

Just like Wonder Woman, (or Superman) you can change your mind and attitude, just like she changed her clothes with a quick twirl. If you find your day suddenly out of control- get alone somewhere (bathroom works) and pull yourself back into that peaceful state with some focused breathing; letting go of the stress with each breath and breathing in peace (throw in a couple of twirls also if you would like)☺

Affirmations: I love mornings. I start my days well. I start my days with great thoughts. I create days of peace. My days are filled with joy. I respond calmly to life. I have great energy for life. I am excited about my life.

Day 38- What Do You Want?

Welcome to day 38- almost there!

Complete this sentence: when I...(insert wish here)...then I will be happy. What people really want is the *feeling* that dream job, relationship or thing will give them. The truth is nothing outside of yourself will give you lasting happiness. Happiness is a choice you can make right now, you can choose to be happy by the selection of thoughts you select. It just may take a little effort. I am not saying to give up on your dreams, but wouldn't it be nice to be content without *needing* to have them? To feel fulfilled and content regardless? Stay with me here.

The problem with needing something to make you happy is it is declaring a "lack," and by saying you lack something actually pushes it away from you. There are millions of us that believed we needed more money, a partner or children to be happy and found that after they came into our lives, we returned to roughly the same level of happiness we were at before. It has apparently been proven that we reset back to our original level of happiness within 1 year of either winning the lottery or becoming a paraplegic. Often the mental energy we used to use to complain about not having, eventually turns into similar energy we now use to complain about the very things/people in our lives we thought we couldn't live without.

Shift away from *need* and having to have something to be happy to "it would be nice" or "I would like," can you hear the shift? By this point of the journey I am optimistic you are feeling a shift internally and reconnecting to self, bringing a greater sense of fulfillment and peace. Instead of feeling lack and need, can you focus on this very moment? Do you have everything you need right now? This moment is all you have, right here, right now.

The irony is the moment we truly let go and say: "if I never get what I think I have to have, I will be happy anyway." The very thing you now *don't need* will probably show up. Because you have shifted out of a desperation for it, it can now come to you. You have essentially created room for it. Every day ask the question: what do I really, really want? And then be thankful for it, trusting it to come.

More joy please...

Your brain has a hard time sorting real from imaginary, that's why we can use different visual activations and techniques to change how we feel. So use your imagination to help you, yes- "fake it until you make it" basically. Use it like a tool to *get* you happy, well its better than the alternative and some of us will take any help we can get!

Picture having what you want and it being in your life right now. Sit with that thought and imagine the feelings as if it was actually your current reality. A better marriage, 4 more zeros on your bank account, the ultimate vacation, whatever it is. How would your life alter? Go about your day and act as if it is so and enjoy the feelings that cultivated, at the same time your circumstances can begin to line up with your new energy. Hope has a feeling, hope keeps you motivated.

Happiness actually comes *before*- it precedes what you want, not the other way around. Don't wait to be happy, go ahead and choose it now and you will attract everything you want into that new magnetic space. When I was in my recruiting job, I would talk to people all the time that were miserable or frustrated because they couldn't get a job and they couldn't get a job because they were miserable and frustrated-it was a catch-22. Or to illustrate my point, their negative energy (thoughts, attitudes, words and behavior) was pushing their next opportunity away from them. Dating is the same way, you have to be relaxed about it and not desperate.

We live by this unspoken law all the time but many people don't want to accept responsibility for their bad energy, but they sure notice other people's negative energy. Even little kids know to avoid their dad when he's in a bad mood. That's also why people are called the "life of the party." That is where everyone wants to be- around the upbeat, fun persons' energy.

This principal is such a game changer- that is why I am repeating it the whole way through this book, this isn't just a bunch of wishful positive rambling, it's how life works. The faster you learn how to play along, the easier life will work for you. Ever wonder why one person's life is like a dream and someone else's is like a nightmare- just look a little closer. You have the power to change the game.

Day 39-Love and Flow

Love is all there is.

We are all One, and we are all connected, so how you treat others is really how you treat yourself and it will absolutely come back, so choose wisely.

Choose love as often as possible, for that is surely what you will get back.

Decide the world is friendly and it will be.

Decide it is hostile and it will be that to you instead.

Treat others as if they *are* you, be as sensitive and kind to others as you would like them to be to you. You can lift the energy of others around you by responding in love and kindness whether they deserve it or not.

I know many out there are struggling to get ahead, be first, get the best parking space and beat you to the door of the restaurant. But instead, believe your timing is perfect, and that there is more than enough. Stay in the natural flow of life, like the river moving down stream around the rocks with no stress, no resistance- it simply trusts the process of life. Be like the water. It can be a challenge to stay in that flow, but as you practice it gets easier and you won't be as easily rattled. Surrender every day, recognize your ego fighting for its survival and live out of your heart (your peaceful center) more than your head. Give up the struggle and find your flow every day, the best way to do that is to surrender to it, give up the battle and be at peace.

Today declare, "I surrender" and let go of any stress (fear), move with life not against it. Come from a place of trust, peace and inner rest, refusing to get upset by life and its challenges.

I realize sometimes life requires struggle: giving birth, starting a new business or winning at sport. But for the most part, find your place of peace inside and operate out of that. Don't operate out of your ego, give up the need to fight, and struggle to get ahead in life.

Give love out in its many forms: in genuine interest, eye contact, a warm hug, be generous with it and you will get it back in equal measure.

You may be thinking this all sounds very "peace and love" but let's face it the Hippies were right, all you need is love and out of that flows, peace and joy, bottom line you will be happier- and it works. All of life is choice, you were given free will to choose, and you can choose to be whatever you want today- miserable or happy absolutely up to you.

You can still be assertive, you don't have to be a doormat. Most drama can be avoided by not engaging, it's hard to fight with only one person involved.

Love on purpose...

Any day you think of it you can ask: "who is my person today?" Who can you encourage, or help in some way? Get still for a moment and let a face or a name come to you. If it seems blank, maybe it's a stranger you haven't met yet, or maybe you are your person for that day.

Day 40- Laugh!

Welcome to day 40- you made it!

Today is about enjoying the journey.

Go ahead and bask in the satisfaction of completing this life changing process.

Laugh often, and at every opportunity, laugh right in the face of frustrations and irritations.

The most enlightened folks to walk our planet believe: nothing bad is happening to them, everything is working for their greater good and they are completely safe- even in death. You can choose to believe that too if you like? What a world it would be if we all trusted to that degree.

Your life may not look perfect right now, but can you see the perfection in it? It is okay if you aren't exactly where you expected to be by this age or stage of life. Shitty days happen, just don't give up when they do. Shake it off, keep good habits going and things will move in the right direction.

You are doing your best, which doesn't require you to have it all mapped out perfectly. You are far more unique and interesting than that.

You are awake now, don't go back to sleep but continue to grow as you journey on into greater and deeper of all that life has for you.

I know it was challenging at times throughout this process, but you did it, you made it!

Can I say- I am proud of you ☺

If you would like to share any part of your journey through this work, I would love to hear from you.

Email: (the book title) 40daystoemotionalfreedom@gmail.com

Website: www.maryannerodgers.com

Look out for my web page: 40 Day Finishers: set up for anyone who finishes this journey.

Be well,
Maryanne

ABOUT THE AUTHOR

Maryanne Rodgers is a Life Coach living in Southern California with her husband Randy and dog Chuckles. Maryanne is originally from New Zealand, born to an Irish father and New Zealand mother, raised with her sister Lisa. Maryanne moved to the US in 2000, and comes from a career background in IT Recruiting, as well as prior experience in childcare and elderly care.
Apart from writing, Maryanne enjoys relaxing with family and friends, walking Chuckles at the beach, and the occasional game of Texas Holdem.

www.ingramcontent.com/pod-product-compliance
Lightning Source LLC
Chambersburg PA
CBHW062026040426
42447CB00010B/2158